Assertiveness for Men

Stop Being a Pushover and Learn to Say No by Using These Proven Techniques

By

John Adams

© Copyright 2018 - All rights reserved.

The content contained within this book may not be reproduced, duplicated or transmitted without direct written permission from the author or the publisher.

Under no circumstances will any blame or legal responsibility be held against the publisher, or author, for any damages, reparation, or monetary loss due to the information contained within this book. Either directly or indirectly.

Legal Notice:
This book is copyright protected. This book is only for personal use. You cannot amend, distribute, sell, use, quote or paraphrase any part, or the content within this book, without the consent of the author or publisher.

Disclaimer Notice:
Please note the information contained within this document is for educational and entertainment purposes only. All effort has been executed to present accurate, up to date, and reliable, complete information. No warranties of any kind are declared or implied. Readers acknowledge that the author is not engaging in the rendering of legal, financial, medical or professional advice. The content within this book has been derived from various sources. Please consult a licensed professional before attempting any techniques outlined in this book.

By reading this document, the reader agrees that under no circumstances is the author responsible for any losses, direct or indirect, which are incurred as a result of the use of the information contained within this document, including, but not limited to, — errors, omissions, or inaccuracies.

Table of Contents

Chapter 1: Introduction to Communication Styles   7
    Passive Communication   8
    Aggressive Communication   10
    Passive-Aggressive Communication   12
    Assertive Communication   14

Chapter 2: Why Do We Behave the Way We Do?   17
    Reasons for Aggressive Behavior in Men   18
    Reasons for Passive-Aggressive Behavior in Men   20

Chapter 3: Current Level of Assertiveness   25
    Questionnaire #1 to Identify Your Current Level of Assertiveness   25
    Questionnaire #2 to Identify Your Current Level of Assertiveness   30
    Assertiveness Journal to Know Your Current Status   31

Chapter 4: Building Assertiveness Based On Your Core Values   33
    Importance of Core Values   33
    Discovering and Defining Core Values   34
    Core Values and Assertiveness   37

Chapter 5: Change Your Inner Beliefs   39
    Assertive Rights   40
    Changing Your Inner Beliefs   41

Chapter 6: Communication Techniques to Practice   47
    Tips to Improve Assertiveness in Your Communication   48
    Assertive Communication and Handling Criticism   52
    Final Wrap-Up Practice Tips for Assertiveness   54

Chapter 7: Tools to Build Assertiveness 55
    Power Poses to Increase Assertiveness 57

Conclusion 61
    Assertive People are Winners and Learners 61

    Assertive People are Loved by All 61

    Assertive People are Amazing Communicators 61

    Assertive People Tend to have Healthy, Happy Relationships 62

    Assertive People have High Self-Esteem and Confidence 62

    Assertive People Know the Power of Emotions 63

Chapter 1: Introduction to Communication Styles

What is assertiveness? It is a type of personality trait typically reflected through outward behavior and communication. A man who is assertive is one with the power to stand up for his own rights and those of others. The primary element that differentiates assertiveness from other forms of behavior and communication is the articulation of one's rights without subjugating or hurting other people in the process.

Even in the midst of an intensely conflicting argument, an assertive man will never say or do anything that offends or upsets the opposing party. In a calm and composed demeanor, he will talk about his own opinions and beliefs. Assertiveness is the perfect balance between aggression and passiveness. Therefore, assertiveness can be defined as a personality trait that empowers a man to express his opinion, beliefs, thoughts, and feelings, honestly and directly.

It is a good idea to start understanding the concept of assertiveness and how to go about building it by learning the basics about the four different primary communication styles, including:
1. Passive
2. Aggressive
3. Assertive
4. Passive-Aggressive

Passive Communication

Passive communication refers to a style in which people do not openly express their opinions, feelings, and thoughts. People with a passive communication style don't stand up and fight for their rights. They also cannot stand up for other people's rights. Typically, passive communication is associated with low self-esteem, driven by a feeling of being useless and worthless. Passive communicators are people who think that they deserve the punishments and ill-treatment they get.

Therefore, passive communicators do not react to hurtful or angry sentiments made against them. Instead of expressing their feelings, passive communicators accumulate negativities inside themselves. However, it is not possible to hold on forever. Each of us has a threshold point, and when that point is breached, the suppressed negativities burst forth in unpleasant and even dangerous ways.

Characteristics of Passive Communicators:

Bashful – Nearly all passive communicators are shy by nature and will not raise their voice to say something even if they don't like it. For example, if your boss is continuously loading you up with excess work while letting many others off, and you are not saying anything about the situation, then you are a passive communicator. Shyness prevents you from drawing attention to yourself. You simply choose to be agreeable.

Highly sensitive – Almost all passive communicators are sensitive to criticism. For example, if your boss says something like, "You must do something about your tardiness," and you take this statement to heart and feel sad and hurt, then you could have a passive communication style.

Self-conscious – Passive communicators are self-conscious of how they come across to people. This deep sense of self-consciousness is one of the primary reasons passive communicators have difficulty expressing their opinions and feelings.

All these characteristics result in depression, anxiety, and feelings of inadequacy and immaturity in passive communicators.

Examples of typical passive communicator responses and scenarios:

- I cannot say anything to my boss; I will lose my job
- I am only smart enough for this level of work; I am not worthy of a promotion
- No one loves me; I am all alone in this world
- I cannot ask that beautiful girl out for a date because I am ugly
- You visit a restaurant, and the steak you ordered is not to your satisfaction. When the waiter asks for feedback, you tell him everything is all right

Challenges faced by passive communicators:

- People will never care for your views and opinions
- You will be overlooked for promotions and bonuses
- You will be taken for granted, and unreasonable expectations will be placed on you
- Accumulation of undue stress and anxieties could lead to depression

Mao Zedong, the founding father of the People's Republic of China, said, *"Passivity is fatal. We aim to make our enemies passive!"*

Aggressive Communication

Aggressive communicators are the exact opposite of passive communicators. They voice their opinions, feelings, and thoughts so forcefully that it hurts and violates the rights of other people.

Characteristics of Aggressive Communicators:

They do not listen – Aggressive communicators rarely make an effort to listen during a conversation. Here, we are not just talking about the absence of active listening. The basic attention required to be given to someone who is talking is also missing.

Thus, aggressive listeners only project their own viewpoints, resulting in a one-way monologue instead of a healthy conversation. Moreover, if other participants do manage to voice their opinions, they are ruthlessly and forcefully rejected without rhyme or reason.

Aggressive communicators only pursue personal goals – The absence of listening during a conversation is driven by a personal agenda. Aggressive communicators typically seek just their own goals. They want only to transmit messages that meet their personal goals, and everything else is aggressively and forcefully relegated to the background.

Aggressive communicators rarely speak to interact or share information with others. They only want to voice their opinion and crush the voices of everyone else in the group.

They lack empathy – The absence of listening, and the sole purpose of pursuing personal goals, combine to render aggressive communicators as totally unempathetic. All others' thoughts, feelings, and emotions are insignificant before their own.

All these characteristics make aggressive communicators come across as violent, rude, nasty, dominating, and insensitive.

Examples of typical aggressive communicator responses and scenarios:

- I am superior to you
- I am right, and you are wrong
- I will get my way, no matter what
- I can infringe upon your rights
- You owe me
- Everything is your fault

Challenges faced by aggressive communicators:

- Alienated by friends and family
- Everyone will avoid talking or interacting with them
- Despite having great oratory skills, they can never win an argument because they will never be invited for a

discussion
- If they are in a position of power, then people will hate and fear them
- If they have no power, then they will be ridiculed, mocked, or worse still, completely ignored

Jose Mourinho, the famed Portuguese football manager, said, "The world today is so competitive, selfish, and aggressive that during the time we spend in this world, we must try and be everything but that."

Passive-Aggressive Communication

People with a passive-aggressive communication style are those that appear passive on the outside but are deeply aggressive on the inside. Can you think of anybody in your office whom the boss insults and humiliates? Maybe the person smiles and tries to brush off the insult, and later on tells you, in secret, that, henceforth, he is going to make life hell for his boss. That is an example of a passive-aggressive kind of behavior.

What about your dealings with your children? You are ordering them to clean their rooms, and you can hear them mutter their resentment under their breath. When you ask them to talk loudly, they simply turn around, smile, (falsely, most of the time) and say, "Nothing!" This is another classic case of passive-aggressive behavior. It is a combination of the fear of openly antagonizing authority and the deep urge to be aggressive too. They react in such a way that you cannot find a fault, and yet you know that such people are behaving in a passive-aggressive manner.

Characteristics of Passive-Aggressive Communicators:

They often use the silent treatment – The silent treatment is one of the most standard reactions used by passive-aggressive communicators. Completely ignoring someone is not really passive-aggressive, as it is an explicit behavior. For example, there could be a coworker who 'accidentally' doesn't see you in the hallway when you greet him. When you remind him, he simply says he didn't see.

They use subtle insults – For example, a colleague could say something nice to you in front of others, for which you might even thank him. However, when you think about it later, you realize that the compliment was an insult in disguise.

Sulking behavior – Sulking and being grumpy is typical of teenage passive-aggressive behavior. You refuse to give your son permission for a night out with his friends. Sulking, being grumpy, not sitting at the table to have dinner with the rest of the family, etc., are classic cases of passive-aggressive behavior.

Vengeful – A passive-aggressive person will not forget the pain and agony of not having the strength to fight back, so he chooses to find deceptive ways of taking revenge. For example, it is possible that a resentful subordinate will secretly go behind your back to your boss to complain about you.

Examples of typical passive-aggressive communicator responses and scenarios:

- *I am not mad* – This is, perhaps, the most common response from a passive-aggressive communicator. Even when directly asked to express his feelings, this person will not, and instead will seethe within himself.
- *Fine! Whatever!* – Classic phrases of sulking behavior
- *I am coming* – Verbally, they will be heeding orders, but they will use every delay tactic to put off implementing the orders
- *You always find a fault with me* – A typical response by teenage children when asked to clean the room or improve their grades

Challenges of passive-aggressive behavior

- Such individuals remain stuck with their negative emotions; in fact, such people are at a higher risk of becoming depressed because the accumulation of negative energy stem from two sources; from being aggressive and from being passive
- They might resolve their immediate resentment through underhanded means, but the root problem remains unresolved
- Passive-aggressive people's true personalities come out sooner, rather than later, and they become alienated from people

Assertive Communication

An assertive communication style is one that helps you balance the passive and aggressive styles. An assertive person will state his feelings, thoughts, and opinions firmly, but without violating the rights and beliefs of other people. Abraham Lincoln said, *"Those who deny freedom to others do not deserve it themselves."* Therefore, an assertive man is one who will say what he wants to say and allow others to state their opinions too.

Characteristics of Assertive Communicators:

Respectful behavior – Assertive people respect everyone involved in a conversation and value all comments and remarks

Sincere interaction – Unlike passive-aggressive communicators, whose outer behavior does not align with their inner personality, assertive communicators say what they feel, without any pretense.

Value and accept themselves – This approach gives assertive people self-confidence that is rooted in self-awareness and not in arrogance. They accept themselves for their strengths and weaknesses.

Excellent emotional stability and self-control – Assertive people know how to manage their emotions, which helps them handle the most intense arguments, calmly and composedly.

Excellent communication skills – Assertive people work on their communication skills and are always working to develop and improve them. They understand the importance of communication for great interpersonal relationships and success.

Examples of typical assertive communicator responses and scenarios:

- I am confident of myself, but I also know you could be right in your perspective
- We are all entitled to our views, opinions, and thoughts
- I speak with honesty and clarity
- I get straight to the point and avoid beating around the bush
- I value my personal rights and will not let anyone violate them. I also respect and honor the individual rights of others.

Benefits of assertive communication:

- You will earn the respect of your colleagues, boss, and coworkers
- Your family will also love and respect you for what you are
- As you will be focused on addressing core issues in your life, you will mature and develop as a human being
- You will be quite popular and well-liked by most people because of your ability to respect everyone

Generally, women are considered to be less assertive than men, although this trend is changing radically in the modern world. This outlook actually puts more pressure on men because they are expected to already be in possession of this skill. Irrespective of your level of assertiveness, the good thing is that you can improve on it and get better at it through diligent practice and hard work. The art of assertiveness will give you a big edge in this rather competitive world.

Chapter 2: Why Do We Behave the Way We Do?

The idea of aggressive and passive-aggressive behaviors in modern times is not very difficult to explain and understand. There is a lot of pressure in the modern world to behave appropriately and not let emotions overtake and overwhelm us. Therefore, even as children, we are taught to suppress emotions, especially negative ones, so that we look "dignified" and "civilized." Many of us are trained to believe that suppressing emotions is the most effective way of handling them.

However, that is not really true. Our emotions work in tandem with our intelligence to help us understand the world and its happenings. Emotions orchestrate our lives. Sometimes, the resultant music can be a sad and depressing tune, while, at other times, it may be happy and refreshing.

An old Arab proverb goes something like this: "A man who cannot understand the look can never comprehend the explanation." Emotions speak a universal language and bind human beings together. It is unfortunate that such a beautiful element of human beings is being suppressed instead of being used effectively.

Moreover, emotions are nothing but energy that helps us manage the ups and downs in our lives. Suppressing emotions is equivalent to locking up the energy inside our system. The more we suppress our emotions, the more they accumulate in our body and mind. This accumulation of energy is called the "percolator effect."

Percolators are used to make coffee. You put in the coffee powder, add some water, and switch on the machine. The energy from the coffee is released and accumulates inside the percolator, allowing the coffee to brew perfectly. If you don't let the steam from the machine out at the right time, it will burst forth, spewing hot coffee all over you.

Similarly, our emotions are being "brewed" inside our body, and we need to find suitable exits for the emotions so that our lives turn out as perfectly-balanced coffee, poured from a well-maintained percolator. Mature expressions of emotions are the healthiest way of releasing them from our systems. Instead, if we suppress and accumulate them, they will burst forth when the threshold of repressed emotions is breached, ending up spewing venom all around. The result of repressed emotions can be devastating for everyone involved.

Aggressive people use violent and nasty ways to express their emotions while passive-aggressive people use underhanded ways of dealing with their emotions. Both these methods are not only ineffective ways of releasing emotional energy from our system but also have harmful and dangerous consequences, as discussed in Chapter 1.

Reasons for Aggressive Behavior in Men

Identifying the underlying causes of aggressive behavior will help you manage your communication style better than before. There are some scientifically proven reasons for aggressive behavior in men:

The brain of a man is not wired for empathy – Multiple research studies have revealed that the male brain is not really wired for empathy. It is more wired for problem-solving than trying to listen to and relate to underlying emotions. This is one of the reasons why your wife is constantly complaining that you don't listen to her problems. The instant she starts complaining, your brain is hardwired to find solutions for her, and all she wants is for you to listen to her. Stopping her in midsentence is the most primal and basic form of aggression.

Men have higher levels of testosterone – Higher levels of testosterone are directly connected to aggressive and violent behavior. While genetic factors play a role in the amount of testosterone in your system, the social and physical conditions around you also play a critical role. When your life is strengthened through strong familial bonds, and you surround yourself with loving friends and family, then your testosterone levels decrease, thereby lowering your urge for aggression.

Men have lower levels of oxytocin – Studies have revealed that people with higher levels of oxytocin are friendlier, more trusting, more empathetic, and less aggressive than people with lower levels of oxytocin, a chemical that is naturally produced in our body. Oxytocin generates a feeling of empathy, resulting in gentle behavior. Additionally, testosterone is known to block the functioning of oxytocin.

The good thing for men is that it is relatively straightforward to raise oxytocin levels. Regular massages are known to increase oxytocin levels. You could also make a conscious effort to trust other people instead of being fearful and defensive.

Unresolved childhood problems such as trauma,

abuse, and more – The sudden death of a loved one, parents who were always fighting with each other, or physical, sexual, or emotional abuse during childhood are personality-affecting incidences. If these issues remain unresolved, then their negative impacts in adulthood will result in aggressive behavior.

Low self-esteem – One of the most significant contributing factors to aggressive behavior is low self-esteem. Men who feel unworthy and unloved use aggressive behaviors to cover up their inner feelings.

Reasons for Passive-Aggressive Behavior in Men

The only difference between aggressive and passive-aggressive behavior is the manifestation of aggression. Aggressive men tend to openly resist authority or use discernible ways to show their aggression. Passive-aggressive men, on the other hand, choose more subtle ways of showing their aggression. Here are some reasons why some men choose passive-aggression over aggression:

Showing negative emotions is not socially acceptable – Modern society treats displays of anger with disdain. As already mentioned earlier, we are trained to suppress emotions, rather than show or express them. Expressing emotions maturely is a sign of assertiveness, a quality that non-assertive men lack. Therefore, to appear compliant with accepted social norms, they tend to act in a passive-aggressive way.

It is easy to get away with passive-aggressive

behaviors – Passive-aggressive behaviors ride on the thin line separating the two extremes between passivity and aggression. So, bad behavior in passive-aggressive men is difficult to differentiate from open aggression which helps them get away with it.

For example, if your boss tells you to do something, and you whisper your resentment under your breath instead of openly being aggressive, then that is showing passive-aggression. When your boss, who knows you've said something, challenges you to speak your thoughts, you can choose to say, "Nothing, boss!" Easy to get away with.

Getting revenge is one of the most wonderful things to happen – Passive-aggressive people are typically out to get revenge for their humiliation or feelings of being insulted. In fact, aggressive people really don't care about revenge because they have already managed to strangle other people's opinions and views while forcefully presenting their own ideas. Aggressive people do end up expressing their feelings, even if wrongly and damagingly.

On the other hand, passive-aggressive people are not able to express their emotions, openly resulting in vengefulness. For example, your boss asks you to do a presentation that you don't really want to do. You swear under your breath, put on a false smile for him, and grudgingly take on the task.

The way to get revenge is to do a shoddy job with your presentation. You have followed your boss' orders outwardly, but he knows, and you know that shoddy work requires him to redo the entire thing. And he cannot even be angry because you can say that you did what you believed you thought was right. A perfect and classic example of passive-aggressive behavior!

Passive-aggressive behavior gives you satisfaction (even if only cursory) of expressing your resentment or anger without the responsibility of the consequences that come with aggressive behavior. In many ways, passive-aggressive behaviors are more dangerous and unpleasant than aggressive behaviors. In the latter, there is at least a sense of openness involved, with little or no guile.

Examples of Famous People Who Did Not Need Aggression

One of the most common reasons given by men for their aggression is that they believe they require this trait to be successful. Such men believe that leaders and famous people are seen to be loud, needlessly emphatic, and aggressive. Nothing is farther from the truth than this concept. Here are some examples of famous people and great leaders who never need aggression to achieve success:

Tom Hanks – This Hollywood superstar who could, perhaps, get away with aggressive behavior, thanks to his overwhelming global popularity, is a super-nice man who chooses to typewrite responses to every fan letter on beautiful stationery. He treats every opinion and feedback with dignity and honor.

Sigmund Freud – The father of psychoanalysis did not only treat famous and rich people. A distraught mother of a gay individual wrote to him, begging him to "cure" her son of homosexuality. This happened when a large portion of the American population was blaming the gay community for causing the Great Depression. The letter he wrote to this lady was way ahead of its time when he explained the naturalness of her son's state of mind.

The detailed letter reflects Sigmund Freud's painstaking efforts to understand the lady's and her son's pain and help them overcome it. Another great example of how great men do not need aggression to become popular and famous.

Stan Lee of Marvel Comics – Today, Stan Lee is nothing short of being a god to comic lovers across the globe. However, way back in 1947, he was still a novice in the industry and was working as a junior editor with *Timely Comics*, the precursor to *Marvel Comics*. During that time, he wrote a little book called *Secrets Behind the Comics* in which he promised to edit and review any reader's aspiring work of comic art for a sum of $1.

Now, cut to 1972. Russell Maheras was a budding comic artist, while Stan Lee had grown by leaps and bounds in his career and was the editor-in-chief of Marvel Comics. Russell Maheras had a copy of Stan Lee's 1947 book. He sent a copy of his comic art, which he called *Superman*, along with the required dollar amount, to Stan Lee for his review, reminding him of the promise he'd made to all his readers way back in 1947.

And true to his word (despite having the luxury of getting away without heeding the request), Stan Lee sent back a detailed editor's note to Russell Maheras, praising him highly for certain elements and critiquing him for others! An assertive, promise-delivering gentleman to the core!

If you are an aggressive or passive-aggressive person, and you are slowly but surely realizing the disadvantages and futility of such behaviors, then you don't need to fret. The desire to change is the first and most important step in a positive direction. With tips, suggestions, and recommendations from this book, you can easily turn over a new leaf to build and develop assertiveness.

Chapter 3: Current Level of Assertiveness

'When I discover who I am, I'll be free," said Ralph Ellison, one of America's most influential scholar, literary critic, and novelist.

This chapter is dedicated to helping you become self-aware; to help you understand how assertive you are right now. The questions are based on the self-expression scale taken from *The College Self-Expression Scale*, published by John P. Galassi and others in 1974.

The questions are phrased to elicit a "Yes" or "No" answer from you. In the end, count the number of "yesses" and "nos." The "yesses" reflect your assertiveness and the "nos" reflect the lack thereof.

Questionnaire #1 to Identify Your Current Level of Assertiveness

Q1. Suppose you are standing in line at a bank that has four people in front of you and three more after you. Another man walks in, skips the line, and goes straight to the teller to get his work done. He does not even glance at the people waiting in line. Will you tell this man to go back and take his rightful place at the end of the line? Y/N

Q2. You buy your wife a lovely new dress from a shopping mall, located some distance away from your home. The person who serves you promises that everything is all right with the dress and that she has checked it. Your wife, however, finds a little tear near the sleeve. Will you go back to the store, register a complaint, and get an exchange? Y/N

Q3. You and your colleague have a big argument about a joint presentation you have to prepare for the CFO's visit in 10 days' time. The argument is about how to make it most effective. You have a viewpoint, and your colleague has something entirely different. You win the battle, and the first draft of the presentation (which took up three days of work) is completed and taken to your boss for approval. He takes one look at it and disapproves of it immediately. He further explains how the presentation should be done, which is exactly what your colleague was talking about. Will you accept your mistake and apologize to your colleague? Y/N

Q4. If you are angry with your children or your wife, do you express your anger in a straightforward and upfront manner, supporting your emotion with suitable reasons? Y/N

Q5. Your best friend of many years has been borrowing small amounts of money from you lately, without returning it most of the time. This time he has asked for a relatively large amount of money. Will you turn him down, citing honest reasons regarding his lack of intention to repay the amounts borrowed earlier? Y/N

Q6. In any group conversation, do you take care to draw out quiet people and ensure that you listen to and honor everyone's point of view and opinions? Y/N

Q7. In group conversations, do you make an effort to voice your opinions and views firmly, but take care not to hurt or violate other people's rights? Y/N

Q8. Are you comfortable openly asking for favors from your friend(s)?

Q9. You have finally gotten this beautiful hot girl from your office to go on a date with you. You have chosen a fairly pricey, high-end restaurant for your dinner. You are leaving no stone unturned to show your date how sophisticated and suave you are. Your dinner arrives, and the steak is not cooked the way you asked for it. Although your date has asked for the same thing, she doesn't seem too upset about her food. Will you call the waiter and express your disappointment? Y/N

Q10. You are planning to accessorize your new car but need to be under a strict budget. The salesman at the accessory shop is showing you fabulous add-ons for your car which are way above your budget. Will you be able to say no to the salesman and stick to the most basic accessories within your budget? Y/N

Q11. Your teenage child is studying for his upcoming SAT exams next week. It's a weekend and a few of your friends arrive, unannounced, to spend the day with you. They are great friends. But the noise of all of you guys together is definitely going to disturb your son. Will you politely tell your friends to go away now and choose another more convenient day for the day-long party? Y/N

Q12. Are you comfortable sharing your views and opinions with your friends and family members? Y/N

Q13. Are you comfortable sharing your views and opinions with your office colleagues and the people in your professional circle? Y/N

Q14. You are in the middle of a meeting in which your boss is making a presentation. Suddenly he says something that you know to be incorrect. Your boss's boss is also present in the meeting. Will you stand up and correct him? Y/N

Q15. An old and respected ex-boss visits you for dinner. You owe this man a lot because he taught you the tricks of the trade when you started in the profession. Now he says something that you strongly disagree with. Will you politely say so and offer a counterpoint? Y/N

Q16. You go to the local hardware store to buy some nails. You take the change, without counting it, and walk out. On the way home, you notice that you have been short-changed. Will you walk back and request the correct change? Y/N

Q17. An old buddy who has helped you many times before with loads of money now comes to you with an unreasonable, even immoral, request. Will you stand up to him and say no? Y/N

Q18. Your favorite sister, who is going through a terrible divorce, wants to take up residence in your house which is already quite small for the four of you, including your wife and two kids. Will you tell her so and help her find other accommodation? Y/N

Q19. You are playing a baseball game with some boys in the neighborhood. It's a team of adults vs. kids. Nearly all the adults are professional players, including you. The kids are not professionals. But they are young, energetic, and quick to learn. They seem to be winning the game. You notice a close friend indulging in some underhanded dealing which results in your team winning the game. Will you stand up and question your friend? Y/N

Q20. You are going steady with a girl, and it almost seems that both of you might get married. Wanting to be upfront with her, you choose to tell her some closely-guarded secrets, including some embarrassing ones involving your friends. She goes around spreading what she has heard from you, and everyone in the neighborhood has a good laugh at you and your friends. Will you raise your voice against this betrayal and leave your girlfriend? Y/N

Q21. You are waiting in a line at one of the cash counters in a department store when you notice the billing clerk attending to someone who was not standing in the line. Will you go to the store manager and complain? Y/N

Q22. When you are in dire straits, do you feel comfortable taking financial help from friends and family? Y/N

Q23. Most of the time, you can laugh at yourself. However, today, there is this one colleague who is mocking you far more than normal, despite you telling her that she has crossed the line of decency. Will you stand up and voice your resentment? Y/N

Q24. You have arrived late for an important office meeting which has already begun. Will you walk up to the front row and take your seat without feeling uncomfortable? Remember, you also have the option of sitting inconspicuously in any of the last rows. Y/N

Q25. You are discussing an important upcoming project with

your team member and your boss walks in, demanding that he speak to you immediately. Will you politely tell him that you will go to his office after finishing the ongoing project discussion with your team members? Y/N

Q26. Are you comfortable being assertive? Y/N

Questionnaire #2 to Identify Your Current Level of Assertiveness

Choose the appropriate answer from the options given to each of the following questions:

Q1. Someone aggressively moves ahead of you while you are standing patiently in line. What do you do?
1. Give the person the benefit of the doubt and gently tell him that there is a line to be followed
2. Look at him angrily but say nothing. Instead, push him "accidentally" and take your rightful place
3. Do or say nothing
4. In a firm tone, tell the person to go back to his correct place in the line

Q2. Your friend is coming over to work on an office project over the weekend. He is supposed to be there by 9:00 a.m., but he only comes in at 10:00. What will you do?
1. Be rude with him and tell him you don't like this kind of undisciplined behavior
2. Keep quiet about the whole thing because you don't like conflicts
3. Ask him politely for the reason for his delay and let him know not to repeat it again
4. You leave the house at 9:30 so that he doesn't find you when he arrives

Assertiveness Journal to Know Your Current Status

Another great way to find your current level of assertiveness is by maintaining a journal. For about a fortnight to a month, maintain a journal in which you write down daily experiences and encounters where you were assertive and not so assertiveness.
- Did you say what you wanted to say?
- What was your communication style?
- What were the feelings going on in your mind?
- Did you manage your emotions without allowing them to overwhelm you?
- Was the outcome of the event directly affected by your ability/inability to handle your emotions?
- Can you identify areas in which you could have behaved in a different way to achieve a better result? What are these areas, and how you could have done better?

When you're making these entries in your journal, remember not to judge yourself. After all, the event is over and done with. You are only looking at learning critical lessons. Have an objective outlook and make detailed notes in your journal on a daily basis.

Use the three tools given in this chapter to correctly gauge your current level of assertiveness and any necessary areas of improvement. You can start working on your self-assertiveness skills from that point.

Chapter 4: Building Assertiveness Based On Your Core Values

Mahatma Gandhi said, "Your beliefs become your thoughts. Your thoughts become your words. Your words become your actions. Your actions become your habits. Your habits become your values. Your values become your destiny."

What is the meaning of core values and what is their importance in one's life? We will start this chapter by answering these questions before moving on to how to identify your core values. What are the core values? They are personal qualities or traits that guide us in our path to our goals. Core values are ideas that enhance the worth of our lives and give them a solid structure.

When we don't have core values, we end up simply drifting through our lives in the direction we are pulled. The best part is that we can define our own core values depending on our personality makeup, our upbringing, our culture, our future goals, and more. What is the importance of defining core values?

Importance of Core Values

Core values give us a sense of purpose – Core values act as an inner compass for our life choices. They help us make decisions based on our own needs instead of drifting along our life path based on external factors such as social and situational pressures. Without core values, we lead our lives to fulfill the needs of others instead of our own. Core values help us lead our own lives instead of living someone else's. Therefore, these values give us a sense of direction and purpose which, in turn, results in happiness.

Core values facilitate making the right choices – Well-defined core values help us make the right choices in our life. Without core values, we could end up making choices that directly conflict with our needs. Moreover, making choices becomes simpler than before because we have only to follow our internal compass. When we are faced with a dilemma, all we need to do is opt for the choice that is aligned with our core values.

Core values make us confident – When we have something of value to guide our lives, we are filled with confidence. Core values give us the courage and confidence to lead our lives in the "right" way.

Discovering and Defining Core Values

There are over 400 core values from which you can choose the ones that you want to define your life's path. Some of them include spirituality, independence, humor, growth, happiness, power, progress, self-reliance, success, forgiveness, and many, many more.

However, instead of choosing from an arbitrary list, it is best to choose from those traits that are already deeply ingrained in our systems. These traits are the ones that we have unwittingly used or not used to make our earlier life choices.

This exercise of discovering and identifying your core values will take a little bit of time and energy, especially if you are doing it for the first time. But it's definitely worth the effort because the outcome of the exercise will be useful throughout your life.

Step 1: Recall the best 4-5 experiences in your life – Reflect on the various events that have happened in your life. Get information from your diary if you have maintained one. Otherwise, simply sit back and jog your memory and think of the top four or five experiences that have given you immense happiness and pleasure. Answer the following questions based on those chosen life experiences:

- What happened? Describe it in detail.
- What were the emotions you felt?
- What were your thoughts?
- Write down the list of personal values that you expressed during the experience. And write down how these values affected your experience

You might have started this exercise with self-doubt, thinking, "how will I remember what happened many years ago?" However, you will realize that many of those happy moments are deeply ensconced in your psyche. When you jog your memory a little bit, you can relive almost the entire experience, especially the emotional memories. Moreover, the values that enhanced the joy of the experience will stand out in your memory.

Step 2: Recall the worst 4-5 life experiences – These memories are typically easy to retrieve because painful memories are more deeply entrenched in our minds than joyful ones. Answer the same set of questions as you did for your best experiences. Only, this time, the last question will be replaced with, "Write down the list of personal values that you were suppressing during the experience. And write down how these values affected your experience."

Step 3: Identify your code of conduct – To arrive at this, you must identify those elements that enhance the value in your life experiences. Think of those elements that come immediately after the basic survival needs of food, clothing, and shelter. These items must be so important to you that, without them, your life will have no meaning whatsoever. In the absence of these elements, you might not die, but you will also not thrive. Examples are:
- A state of continuous learning
- Adventure and thrill
- Financial security
- Family happiness
- Work-life balance
- Good health
- The beauty of nature

Step 4: Group similar values together – Group together similar values from the list you created by following the above three steps. For example, responsibility, timeliness, and discipline can all be grouped together. Similarly, spirituality, prayers, God, and wisdom can be grouped together.

Step 5: Identify the central theme of each group of values – For example, responsibility, timeliness, and discipline could be categorized as "discipline," and the common theme that runs through spirituality, prayers, God, and wisdom is "spirituality."

Step 6 – Make your final list – The number of core values in the final list should ideally be somewhere between five and 10, give or take a few. This number is important to bear in mind while creating your personal list of core values because less than five might not cover all the elements for a meaningful and fulfilling life and more than 10 might be difficult to manage and keep track of.

Step 7 – Rank your final list of core values – This last step in the somewhat big exercise of creating a personal list of core values is bound to take a little more time than you think. Ranking a seemingly equal important list of values can be quite a challenge.
First, rank them as per your gut feel. Sleep on it, and look at the list again the next morning. If your ranking seems fine, then you are most likely on the right path. However, if it feels wrong, then redo the ranking. Repeat until you are satisfied with your list. The ranking is necessary for those occasions when you are in a dilemma that includes two or more values from your own list. At such times, the ranking system gives you amazing clarity on the priorities involved in the dilemma.

Core Values and Assertiveness

Once you have your core values in place and are completely engaged with them, your ability to enhance your level of assertiveness will go up a few notches. While communication is one of the most evident forms of assertiveness, this trait includes a lot more than communication.

Assertiveness is all about core values. In its most wholesome form, assertiveness is a way of life that gives us the power and freedom to live according to our values and principles and not someone else's.
Assertiveness is about accepting ourselves the way we are, including our weaknesses, without feelings of shame or guilt.

In addition to communicating effectively, assertiveness includes:

Keeping our promises – Not keeping our word, or flaking out on our commitments, dents our self-confidence, leading to reduced levels of assertiveness that are driven by low levels of certainty. Core values help you make only those promises that are important in your life; this is an attitude that renders certainty, and therefore self-confidence and assertiveness.

No need to second-guess our choices – A well-drafted core values list, based on increased self-awareness through self-questioning, will ensure that we never have to second-guess our choices, empowering us to be assertive at all times.

Commitment to achieving our goals – Goals are nothing but promises you have made to yourself. So, like keeping your word when you promise something to others, assertiveness helps you keep the promises you make to yourself. Core values play an important role throughout the journey of your goals, right from the time of goal-setting up to their realization.

Defending our beliefs – Being assertive also means standing up for our rights and beliefs if they are in danger of being violated. Core values help us understand and articulate our beliefs, thereby helping us have an increased level of assertiveness.

Therefore, identifying and crystallizing your core values is, perhaps, the first step to increase assertiveness.

Chapter 5: Change Your Inner Beliefs

Our thinking process and the conditioning of our minds is dependent on our inner beliefs. And most of our inner beliefs are already deeply ensconced in our psyche. An important element in your journey to increase your assertiveness is to change your inner beliefs and thought processes. As a grown man, you already have preconceived notions about most of the things and people around you, and about yourself too.
Many of our beliefs are carried forward from our childhood when we were taught certain things. It requires a change in mindset to bring about tangible changes within yourself and the world. For example, until Barack Obama changed his inner belief that an African-American could never become the president of the United States of America and followed through with his goals and visions, all of us believed similarly.

Another classic example of preconditioned inner beliefs is the misconception that outward expressions of anger and sadness are forbidden. Now, as an adult, you know that there are mature ways of assertively expressing anger and sadness. Therefore, this old inner belief is wrong, and you need to change it to live a more meaningful life than before.

Similarly, we must let go and change all those old inner beliefs that have no value today. Here are some more inner beliefs that drive unassertive thinking:
- I must not express my negative emotions because it is wrong to burden others with my problems
- Asserting my ideas and opinions might hurt the other person, and my relationship with that individual will be

ruined
- It is embarrassing to speak about my beliefs and thoughts
- If someone has said "no" to my request for help, then it means that the concerned person does not like or love me
- I do not have to talk about my inner feelings; the people who are really close to me and understand me should be able to read them
- It is selfish to say whatever I want
- Neither I nor anyone else has a right to change their mind
- Ideally, people should keep their emotions to themselves
- If I talk about my nervousness and fear, people will think I am weak and mock me
- If I take praise from others, it means I am arrogant

Assertive Rights

Assertive rights were first published in the 1975 book, *When I say no, I feel Guilty,* written by Manuel J. Smith. He proposed a "bill of assertive rights" which every human being should have. Some of those rights include:
- Everyone, including you, has a right to judge his or her own behavior, emotions, and thoughts and take self-responsibility for the consequences.
- Everyone has a right to say "no"
- No one needs to offer excuses or reasons to justify his or her behavior
- You can judge other people's behavior only if you are responsible for finding solutions to their problems
- Everyone has a right to change his or her mind
- Everyone has a right to disagree with anyone's opinion
- Everyone has the right to make mistakes and accept responsibility for mistakes
- Everyone has the right to say, "I don't know."

- Everyone has the right to be illogical while making choices
- Everyone has the right to say, "I don't understand."
- Everyone has the right to say, "I don't care."

Changing Your Inner Beliefs

So you have to move from unassertive thinking to assertive thinking, and that starts with changing your inner beliefs. But how to go about altering your inner beliefs? The first step to that is to assess your current inner beliefs. Some people might be able to change their way of thinking and their inner beliefs simply by knowing and accepting the assertive right that they have a right to make changes.

However, for some others, this simple technique might not work. They need to challenge their existing inner beliefs head-on, a process called disputation. Disputation is a psychological method of making changes and is based on the idea that our current inner beliefs are primarily learned opinions and not facts. Opinions can be challenged and questioned and need not be blindly followed, especially if they are harming us.

To dispute your thoughts, you need to get to their roots and find evidence for and against those views. Maintaining thought diaries is an effective way to gauge your current beliefs, and then to go about changing them for your own good.

Maintaining thought diaries – The thoughts that run in our minds are random and erratic, and keeping track of them is a huge challenge. Making notes of our thoughts is one of the most effective ways of recalling our thoughts when we need them. Maintaining thought diaries of all your unassertive thoughts will give you a good insight into your current status of inner beliefs.

To make sample entries in your thought diary, let us take an example of a typical friendship scenario. You and your best friends are team leaders managing two different teams within the same department. Both the teams have often helped each other during work overload.

Now, on a particularly difficult day with multiple deadlines hitting your team, you ask your best friend to help. However, he says no. You feel bad about the entire thing and somehow get through the day. You go home and make journal entries in your thought diary.

Part I of the thought diary involves making journal entries regarding your emotions, behavior, and thoughts:

Identifying your emotions – Delve deep into your mind and find answers to the following questions:
What were your feelings? Hurt? Anger? Disbelief? Also rate the intensity of your feelings using numbers 1-10, where 1 stands for least intense and 10 stands for most intense.

_____

Identifying your thoughts – The situation was quite intense. You were already burdened by overwork, and your best friend refused to help. What were the thoughts running through your head?
What were your thoughts? Also rate the intensity of your thoughts using numbers 1-10, where 1 stands for least intense and 10 stands for most intense.

_____

Identifying your behavior – In this intense situation, how did you behave?

What were your physical sensations? What did you do? How did you react/respond? Also rate the intensity of your thoughts using numbers 1-10, where 1 stands for least intense and 10 stands for most intense.

_____

Here are some basic rules to follow when you answer the self-questions on your emotions, thoughts, and behavior:
- Stick only to the facts.
- Don't include your opinions and interpretations. For example, an entry like, "My best friend rudely refused to help me today," is your interpretation. "When I requested help, my friend says no" is factual.
- The rates of the intensity of the emotion, thought, or behavior reflects the strength of your inner belief; the higher the rating you gave, the stronger the inner belief that drives that emotion, thought, or behavior.

Part II of the thought diary – This part has your answers to the following self-responses:
- How can I categorize my behavior? Was I aggressive, passive, passive-aggressive, or assertive?
- Can I identify any evidence for my emotions, thoughts, and behaviors? If yes, what was the evidence?
- Was I ignoring either one of our assertive rights during the event?
- What other perspectives was I missing in the situation?

Here are some sample answers for the two parts of the thought diary of the illustrative experience:
Part I of the thought diary would typically have the following answers:

What were your feelings? *I felt angry and hurt.*
Rate the intensity – *Anger – 8, Hurt – 8*
What were your thoughts? *How could my best friend do this to me? How many times have I helped him, even when I knew I was stretching my team members? How will I meet my deadlines for the day? I always help him whenever he asks.*

Intensity rate - *How could my best friend do this to me? – 9 How will I meet my deadlines for the day? – 8 I always help him whenever he asks – 9*
What were your physical sensations? What did you do? How did you react/respond? – *I did not speak to my friend the entire day after that. When he called me to join him for an evening drink after office hours, I said no.*

Part II of the thought diary would typically have the following entries:

How can I categorize my behavior? Was I aggressive, passive, passive-aggressive, or assertive? *I was passive-aggressive because I chose to ignore him, instead of openly asking him for the reason for his refusal to help.*

Can I identify any evidence for my emotions, thoughts, and behaviors? If yes, what was the evidence? *No, there is no evidence of any kind*

Was I ignoring either one of our assertive rights during the event? *Yes, I was ignoring my right to say no when I chose to help him even when I knew I could not. I was ignoring the rights of my team members when I overworked them for my best friend. By being angry with my friend, I was ignoring his right to say no.*

What other perspectives was I missing in the situation? *The perspectives that I could have missed in my state of high emotion include:*
- My friend's team may already have been overworked
- He might have had a significantly strong and understandable reason to have had to refuse to help me
- There are multiple occasions when I have also said no to him
- I could have thought that this one experience can hardly create a dent in our friendship

How could I have had a more assertive kind of response to the same situation? I could have asked him the reason for his negative response, then and there, instead of sulking.

Now, if you rate the intensity of your emotions and thoughts, you will notice a significant drop. Primarily, you are training your mind not to react and respond based on emotions. You are attempting to change your inner belief that emotions should drive behavior to the idea that objective thinking should drive behavior.

Make multiple entries like this in your thought diary, and keep increasing self-awareness and making changes to your inner beliefs with each lesson.

Chapter 6: Communication Techniques to Practice

Winston Churchill said, "Success is not final and failure is not fatal. What matters is the courage to persist and having the right attitude." You see the power of his communication technique. Just the right words with outstanding impact!

To be able to improve your assertiveness skills in communication, it makes sense to first understand what factors affect the way you communicate.

Reasons for passive communication:
- Overly focused on pleasing everyone except themselves
- Insufficient levels of self-confidence
- Overly anxious about whether their opinions and views will be unacceptable to others
- Intensely sensitive to criticism
- Not building assertive communication skills
- Reasons for aggressive communication:
- Overly focused on achieving one's own desires and needs
- Overconfidence
- Not learning to respect and regard others' opinions and views
- Poor listening skills

Reasons for assertive communication:
Well-developed self-confidence, without arrogance
High level of self-awareness including strengths and weaknesses
Acceptance of who they are

Resilience to criticism and negative feedback
Always in self-improvement mode

Tips to Improve Assertiveness in Your Communication

Say "no" more often – Here are some commonly used assertive responses and phrases that work in many situations. You can learn some of them by rote and use them whenever you have to say no assertively:
- I really appreciate your efforts, but I am not interested at all
- Thanks for the offer, but I cannot make time for this now
- Thanks for your help, but I want to do this on my own
- Thank you very much, but definitely a no (don't forget to smile genuinely with this response)
- Thanks a lot for considering me to be part of your great team, but I'm afraid I will have to pass up the offer this time around.
- Thanks a lot for reaching out to me, but I'm afraid I have a far more important element going on in my life that requires my undivided focus.
- Thank you for your opinion; what do the others in the group think?
- That seems like a good idea. Can I take a couple of weeks to think about it?
- What you're telling me sounds like an urgent request. However, I will not be able to give it that kind of attention right now.
- I don't appreciate your tone of voice (or use of bad language or choice of words)
- Can you please respect and have regard for my perspective

too?
- I felt offended by your behavior
- I understand your love for adventure, but it is not my cup of tea

Practice the right tone of voice – An assertive tone of voice is powerful, strong, and yet calm and friendly. Have you watched Al Pacino in *The Godfather*? Even in the most violent scenes, his tone of voice rings of assertiveness and not aggression! Or for that matter, listen to Morgan Freeman's voice and you can distinctly hear an authoritative ring, cushioned beautifully with a calm demeanor.

You must practice talking aloud to yourself using different tones of voices and see which sounds the best. Your calmness should come from within, which means you must "feel" calm. Here are some tips to improve your tone of voice:

Step 1: Identify those situations when your tone of voice is not natural. Here are a few prompts for you to recall experiences and remember if your voice was "off" during the interaction:
- How comfortable are you in a business meeting setting?
- Are you comfortable sharing your thoughts and ideas in team meetings?
- Do your colleagues respond positively to your ideas when you speak out?
- Are you comfortable talking to your family members? Feel free to break this question up further and ask yourself how comfortable you are talking to your parents, spouse, kids, elders in the family, cousins, siblings, etc.
- Are you comfortable talking to strangers you meet in public places?

Recall your tone of voice in each of these experiences and make a note of those situations when you think it was not right. These are the situations you are uncomfortable in, and so your tone of voice sounds off."

Step 2: Find your casual tone of voice. It is that voice you use to ask someone at your dinner table to pass the salt or pepper. It is your most natural voice. You don't raise your voice, and yet are loud enough for your dining companion to hear from you.

This natural tone of voice is best suited for assertive communication. It is the tone of voice you must use in all situations including your interaction with your wife, parents, coworker, subordinates, and your boss.

Step 3: This "pass the salt" tone of voice is what you need to use in all your uncomfortable situations as well. Recall those uncomfortable situations from Step 1 and, this time, imagine yourself using the "pass the salt" natural tone of voice in each of the situations.

It will take some amount of practice to get over the discomfort of using your natural tone of voice even during uncomfortable situations. Keep rehearsing the uncomfortable situations, speaking aloud to yourself using your natural tone of voice. Initially, speaking emotion-laden words in a natural tone of voice might seem weird. But, with practice, you will realize how much more impactfully assertive your voice sounds when you use your natural tone.

Step 4: Don't hesitate to practice the natural tone in the real-world too. Rehearsing on your own is quite different from speaking in the outside world. So use the first opportunity you get to speak like this in a real scenario. Try it with someone you trust, such as your spouse or your kids or a sibling who is close to you.

Alternately, you can try this "pass the salt" with strangers or billing clerks or a salesperson in a shop. Focus on verbalizing every word deliberately, which will increase the clarity of your speech. With regular practice, you will find yourself habituated into using a natural tone of voice that makes you sound assertive and confident.

Practice listening skills – Assertiveness calls for increased sensitivity to other people's views, opinions, and thoughts. Excellent listening skills are essential for understanding and appreciating others' perspectives. Here are some tips to improve your listening skills and become more assertive than before:

Tip #1: Maintain healthy eye contact with the speaker. Ensure you give your entire attention to the conversation. Working on your computer or looking at your mobile phone while someone is speaking to you is a typical reaction of an aggressive person (if the speaker is your subordinate) or passive-aggressive style (if the speaker holds a higher position than you). Avoid this completely, and maintain eye contact with the speaker throughout the conversation.

Tip #2: Practice paying attention to the speaker without appearing overbearing or anxious. Sometimes when we try to put on an act of paying close attention to the speaker, we might come across as domineering or tense. Be wary of this, and, in a relaxed manner, focus on what the speaker is saying.

Tip #3: Do not judge the speaker. Assertive rights call for you to be open-minded and non-judgmental because everyone has a right to his own opinion or view. This assertive right helps you improve your listening skills as well. Being non-judgmental allows you to listen to what the speaker is saying without malice or mockery and respect him or her for it.

Tip #4: Don't interrupt the speaker and impose your solutions(s) in the midst of the conversation. Interrupting while someone is talking sends the wrong signals and is a typical element of an aggressive communication style. The different messages that a speaker might receive if you interrupt his conversation abruptly include:
- My opinions are more important than yours
- I don't have the energy or the time for your talk
- You are wasting my time
- I don't really care what you think or say

All of us think and speak at different speeds. If you can think and speak faster than your speaker, then it doesn't give you a right to rush her or to stop her midway. Assertiveness calls for you to reduce your speed and align it with that of the speaker so that she and her opinions get the required attention and respect.

Assertive Communication and Handling Criticism

One of the most challenging elements of assertive communication is mastering the art of handling criticism. Here are some tips to help you manage this aspect of assertive communication, depending on the value of the criticism:

Criticism is constructive – Only true well-wishers will take the pains of giving you constructive criticism, facilitating your self-improvement. Therefore, when you know the criticism makes sense and is constructive, accept it wholeheartedly, thank the person, and work on it.

For example, your boss, whom you know has your interests in his heart, finds fault with a presentation that you believed was a great one. Don't get angry with him. Listen to his words attentively, make the necessary changes, and put away the lesson learned for future use.

Criticism is a result of a genuine mistake – If you have made a genuine mistake and someone has found fault with it, don't hesitate to humbly accept your error. Mistakes don't make you a weak or useless person. In fact, accepting your mistake is a sign of courage.

It doesn't matter who has pointed out the mistake. For example, if your subordinate points out an error in your presentation, take it sportingly, thank the person for being so attentive to your presentation, and make the necessary rectifications.

Criticism is unfounded and has no value – One of the best ways to handle negative and valueless criticism is to ignore it completely. However, many times, the criticizer can be nasty enough to say negative things repeatedly. In such circumstances, make sure you tell the person you don't appreciate his or her behavior at all.

Here are some examples of great people who did not let

criticism get in the way of their assertiveness:

Mark Twain - One of the most popular humorists of all time, Mark Twain was heavily criticized for his works. Many critics called his novels vulgar and insensitive. In fact, his most famous work, *The Adventures of Huckleberry Finn*, was criticized as being very un-American. Today, this book is part of many school's academic curricula.

Charles Darwin – It was not easy for this famous scientist to propose his evolution theory based on the survival of the fittest. He faced a lot of criticism from religious believers, and the controversy continues today despite having multiple research studies backing his theory.

Final Wrap-Up Practice Tips for Assertiveness

- Remember, you are as valuable as the people around you
- Before you say anything, ask yourself whether it is fair, respectful, and just
- Don't hesitate or be ashamed to voice your desires, needs, and opinions
- Practice emotion management to help you remain calm and composed in any conversation
- Keep your heart and mind open. Remember that, just because you like or dislike something, everyone shouldn't have to follow your preferences.
- Compliment people openly and heartily
- Take criticism in the right spirit

Chapter 7: Tools to Build Assertiveness

One of the most important elements that reflect your assertiveness is your body language. The use of postures, gestures, the way you present yourself to people, or even a simple handshake can change your communication style from passive to assertive. For example, if you sit up straight in your chair, with your shoulders thrown back confidently, you automatically come across as assertiveness. Contrarily, if you sit with your shoulders slumped, then you appear passive and weak.

Nonverbal communication, of which body language is a critical component, is an essential element of communication. Suppose, for example, that you are giving directions to the cab driver while sitting in the front seat. Now suppose that, mistakenly, you point to the left and say, "Right." The cab driver will turn left, and not right because your hand gesture pointing to the left is far more impactful than your verbal "right."

Body language and nonverbal cues are powerful communication tools. When you are at a negotiating table, you can actually make out the team with the advantage merely by watching the way they sit. The way you sit or stand is communicating something to the other party and the way the other party sits or stands also communicates something to you. Body language is, in fact, a universal language that breaks all geographical and cultural barriers.

Interestingly, in the animal kingdom, body language also seems to play an important role. For example, expanding the chest (as can be seen in gorillas and apes) is a form of dominance over other animals. Basically, animals "open up" by expanding their chest or spreading out their arms or wings to reflect dominance and aggression.

This expansive gesture seems to be present in the human species as well. If you watch a winner crossing the finishing line in a race, or see someone hit a home run, you will see them open out their arms to form a V, their heads up, with their shoulders thrown back. This expansion is a reflection of the power they feel when they win.

On the other hand, have you noticed losers? They sit with their arms wrapped around themselves, their shoulders slouched, and their heads down. It is as if these losers don't want to touch anyone during their moment of powerlessness.

In the same way, have you observed the way you stand with your boss? Unwittingly, you will have complemented his or her power posture. For example, you will have stood next to your boss with your hands folded in and positioned either at the back or in front while your boss stood with his or her arms on her hips or spread out wide. Your boss' expansive power pose is perfectly complemented by your humbling "turned-inward" posture.

Now, take an example when you have called your subordinate to your office to reprimand him for a costly error. Your pose will have been expansive, and your subordinate's pose will have been humbled. This is true most times when two people at different hierarchy levels stand next to each other. Both of them unwittingly complement each other's power poses.

Therefore, we take on a smaller profile when we are next to

someone more powerful than us, and we take on a larger profile when we are next to someone less powerful than us.

Power Poses to Increase Assertiveness

Research studies regarding hormonal levels and assertiveness have made some interesting observations. Assertive people tend to have high levels of testosterone and low levels of cortisol.

Cortisol is a hormone connected to anxiety and stress. Therefore, the lower the level of cortisol, the less the level of anxiety and stress. Testosterone is a hormone directly related to confidence. The higher the level of testosterone, the higher the level of confidence. And this relationship between the two hormones and stress and confidence is seen in both men and women.
Thus, low levels of cortisol and high levels of testosterone enhance confidence, reduce stress and anxiety, and increase assertiveness. Additionally, you will feel more in control of your emotions. Therefore, a balanced amount of cortisol and testosterone can help in improving your assertiveness.

The thing about these two hormones, namely cortisol and testosterone, is that their levels can change rapidly and significantly, depending on the mental, emotional, physical, and environmental cues in and around us. Body language is an important cue that can help manage the levels of these two hormones in our bodies.

One of the most effective poses that help in increasing

assertiveness levels is the "Wonder Woman" pose in which you stand erect with your hands on your hips and your shoulders straight and strong. Standing in this pose for a couple of minutes can help increase your confidence considerably.

For example, if you need to give a presentation, you are nervous despite all your preparation, and you want to increase your feeling of confidence, then this is what you do. Before you enter the room where people are waiting for your presentation, take the "Wonder Woman" pose and stand for a couple of minutes. You will feel more confident than before.

Don't worry about Wonder Woman's name. It is known to be equally effective for men and women. So, go ahead and use it whenever you need to. In fact, it might be a great idea to make the Wonder Woman stance a part of your morning routine. After you brush your teeth, refresh yourself, get dressed, and prepare to leave for your office, take a couple of minutes to stand in front of the mirror in the Wonder Woman pose. It could be a wonderful morning booster to your confidence and assertiveness levels.

Visualization techniques for assertiveness - Visualize assertive behaviors as often as you can. Visualization activates the subconscious mind to generate ideas to be more assertive than before. It programs your brain to recognize and collect the necessary resources needed to become more assertive. It motivates you to increase your assertiveness.

Increased self-awareness for assertiveness – The more you know yourself, the more assertive you can be. Get to know yourself better by writing down your strengths and weaknesses. Next, accept yourself the way you are. Forget about things you cannot control. Work on things you can control, and take the driver's seat in your life.

Love yourself – If you don't love yourself, no one else will love you. Loving yourself is a critical element to becoming more assertive. Learn the art of enjoying your own company. Learn to understand and manage your thoughts. Take care of your physical and mental health. Don't hesitate to pamper yourself regularly.

Each one of us is unique, and it is up to us to find out what makes us unique. Feel the power of this uniqueness and love yourself for it. You will be more in control of your life if you love yourself. And with increased control comes increased assertiveness.

Use the tools and techniques mentioned in this chapter to become more assertive in your life and leverage the multiple effects of assertiveness.

Conclusion

Let us look at the multiple benefits of assertiveness in this final chapter so that you are motivated to reread and redo the questionnaires and exercises in this book and build your assertiveness.

Assertive People are Winners and Learners

Assertive people stand up for their rights and are not scared to fail. They simply use their failures to enhance their learning. Therefore, assertive people are either winners or learners. They are never losers.

Assertive People are Loved by All

Assertive people don't use aggression to say what they want to say. Moreover, they stand up for other people's rights as well. They look upon everyone with respect and dignity. Therefore, assertive people are well-loved.

Assertive People are Amazing Communicators

Assertive people learn the art of great communication, including the use of nonverbal cues. They also understand why assertive communication is the best form of communication. They are aware of their present levels of assertiveness, they know their weaknesses, and they are open-minded to learn and rectify their problems. With the backing of all this knowledge, assertive people become excellent communicators.

Assertive People Tend to have Healthy, Happy Relationships

Excellent communication skills, fantastic ability to voice their own opinions and views without violating the rights of others, and a noble intention to respect and value other people's opinions and views empower assertive people to have healthy, happy relationships that are free from negativities of all kinds. They behave responsibly, handle pressure situations maturely, without being overwhelmed, have no problems in accepting their own mistakes, and are in control of their lives. With all these wonderful traits, assertive people attract a lot of people into their lives and build long-lasting, happy relationships.

Assertive People have High Self-Esteem and Confidence

Assertiveness, confidence, and self-esteem are interminably intertwined, and when one is affected, the other two elements also are impacted in the same way. For example, if you become more assertive than before by practicing and implementing the tips and suggestions in this book, your level of self-esteem and confidence will also see an increase.

Additionally, if you want more detailed information, along with tips and suggestions on self-esteem and confidence, you can choose to buy these books by the same author: *Self-Esteem for Men* and *Confidence for Men*.

Assertive People Know the Power of Emotions

Assertive people are highly self-aware which, in turn, means they know and understand their emotions profoundly and thoroughly. They have learned the art of managing their emotions maturely and prudently, empowering them to handle even stressful situations well.

With this basic idea of assertiveness clearly established in your mind, it is wise to reread and redo the exercises in this book, so you understand yourself even better, and you get on the path of increased assertiveness with confidence and high self-esteem.

If you want to know more about what defines confidence, self-esteem, and assertiveness, and how you can go about building these three critical elements into your personality, then do subscribe to our mailing list to receive useful and informative articles regularly.

www.ingramcontent.com/pod-product-compliance
Lightning Source LLC
Chambersburg PA
CBHW052124110526
44592CB00013B/1740